★ SPORTS STARS ★

SHAQUILLE O'NEAL

SHAQ ATTACK

By Ted Cox

CHILDRENS PRESS ®
CHICAGO

Photo Credits

Cover, 6, ©Barry Gossage; 9, Jonathan Daniel/Allsport USA; 10, AP/
Wide World; 13, ©Barry Gossage; 14, Brad Messina/Louisiana State
University; 16, Reuters/Bettmann; 19, AP/Wide World; 20, Tim Defrisco/
Allsport USA; 23, ©Barry Gossage; 24, Brad Messina/Louisiana State
University; 26, AP/Wide World; 29, Philip Barr/*San Antonio Express-News*;
31, ©Barry Gossage; 32, 35, Brad Messina/Louisiana State University;
37, 38, AP/Wide World; 41, Jonathan Daniel/Allsport USA; 42, 44, ©Barry
Gossage; 47, Jonathan Daniel/Allsport USA

Project Editor: Shari Joffe
Design: Beth Herman Design Associates
Photo Research: Jan Izzo

Library of Congress Cataloging-in-Publication Data

Cox, Ted.
    Shaquille O'Neal : Shaq attack / by Ted Cox.
      p. cm.–(Sports stars)
    Summary: A biography of the basketball player who, in only his second
year as a professional, is being compared to the game's greatest players.
    ISBN 0-516-04379-X
    1. O'Neal, Shaquille–Juvenile literature. 2. Basketball players–
United States–Biography–Juvenile literature. [1. O'Neal, Shaquille.
2. Basketball players. 3. Afro-Americans–Biography.] I. Title. II. Series.
GV884.O54C69   1993
796.323'092–dc20   93-19781
[B]   CIP
                                   AC

SHAQUILLE O'NEAL

SHAQ ATTACK

Nobody has ever come into the National Basketball Association the way Shaquille O'Neal has. There have been big players before, but none as big and as quick as Shaquille. There have been popular players before, but Shaquille created a sensation. You might say he made a big impression.

Shaquille is 7 feet 1 inch tall and weighs just over 300 pounds. That's big, but there have been bigger players. What makes Shaquille great is his quickness—and his desire to improve.

On defense, he jumps high into the air to block shots. On offense, he likes to play low-post center. That means he stands near the basket, with his back to it. His best move, when he gets the ball, is a fast spin around the man guarding him. How did such a big person disappear like that? By the time the opposing center has figured it out, Shaquille is dunking the ball through the hoop.

"He's such a big guy," says Scottie Pippen, a member of the Chicago Bulls and the U.S. Olympic Dream Team. "He's physical. And with his quickness he's very tough to stop inside."

"He brings a new dimension to the game," says NBA Hall of Famer Wilt Chamberlain, a 7-foot-tall former center. "He is electrifying, he is a tremendous shot blocker, and he's extremely graceful and fluid."

"He will be the best," says opposing coach Larry Brown, of the Los Angeles Clippers. "I don't see how other people guard him. He jumps so high and is so strong."

Shaquille (right) and Scottie Pippen

Shaquille plays for the Orlando Magic. He was the first player picked in the 1992 NBA college draft. He signed a contract worth $40 million. Then he went right to work making himself one of the best centers in the NBA.

He is already a very good player. But he wants to get even better. Some people say he could become one of the greatest centers in the history of the game. He is always working to learn and improve. That's what makes him different from a lot of the other rookies who come into the NBA.

That, and his smile. Shaquille has a big smile that curls up at the side, sort of like Elvis Presley's. "He's got it all," says Earvin "Magic" Johnson, the retired Laker great. "He's got the smile, and the talent, and the charisma."

Magic had it all. Michael Jordan has it all. But basketball big men have rarely had it all. People expect them to be great, because of their size. Chamberlain was considered too tall and too good. When he scored 100 points in a single game, some fans said it wasn't fair. Kareem Abdul-Jabbar was another Hall of Fame 7-footer. He set the record for most points scored in a career. But with his unstoppable "sky hook," he made things look too easy. "Nobody roots for Goliath," Wilt Chamberlain once said. Many fans didn't realize how hard Wilt and Kareem had to work to make things look so easy.

Everybody loves Shaq, especially kids.

But everybody loves Shaq, especially kids. They call to him on the street. They yell to him at games during timeouts. Shaq just smiles and winks. Then he listens to what the coach is saying.

"I think I can relate to kids because I'm a kid," says Shaquille. "And I've got younger ones—two younger sisters, a younger brother, a nephew and a niece. I think I know the dos and don'ts of kids."

In 1993, the fans voted Shaq the first rookie since Michael Jordan to start in the All-Star Game. Michael looks at Shaquille and sees someone a lot like himself.

Shaquille shares a laugh with NBA superstar Michael Jordan.

"I think we're people people," says Michael. "We're able to relate with any person. We're kids-oriented. We have good, solid backgrounds with our parents. We've had a lot of parental guidance. We're very outgoing personalities, and we have a very creative type of game."

Being in the NBA spotlight is a lot of pressure for a young person. But Shaquille says, "I don't really think about it that much. I'm the same person. I just keep things simple. I was raised well. I don't hang out in nightclubs. I don't pick fights. I don't drink. I don't shout at people. I'm just going to play hard, and hopefully people are going to like me."

Away from the court, Shaquille is a lot like other young men. He likes cars, and he listens to rap music in his spare time. He says he'd be a rapper if he couldn't play basketball. He probably won't have to worry about that for a while. In fact, he can probably do both. His favorite group is the Fu-Schnickens. He played with them on "The Arsenio Hall Show," and made a music video with them. Shaquille also made plans to do a Hollywood movie.

How does someone like Shaquille keep his feet on the ground, even when they are size 22EE? "It takes a lot to get me excited," says Shaq. "You know what gets me excited? When my mom tells me she loves me. That's the only thing I can think of."

Shaquille rapping on "The Arsenio Hall Show"

Shaquille O'Neal was born March 6, 1972, in Newark, New Jersey. He was the first child of Philip and Lucille Harrison. Philip Harrison liked his wife's maiden name, and so he liked the name they chose for their son. Shaquille O'Neal. It had a ring to it. Little did he know that, someday, millions of people would know that name.

Shaquille's mother told him that his first name meant "Little Warrior." Shaquille would grow up to be a sort of warrior, but he would not be little for long.

Shaquille's father made his career in the
United States Army and became a drill sergeant.
That meant he had to move to a new post every
three years or so. Twice, the Harrisons moved to
Germany and back. That was hard on the family,
but Sergeant Harrison was determined to be a
good father. He wanted his family to be loving
and tight-knit. He wanted his four children to
grow up with solid values.

But all the moving was especially hard on
Shaquille. Even as a child, he was big, and he
felt awkward. "Sometimes, you come into a new
place, and they'll test you," Shaq says. "I always
got tested. Teased about my name. Teased about
my size. Teased about being flunked. You know,
'You're so big, you must've flunked.'"

Shaquille had a bad temper and would
sometimes get into fights over the teasing.
"It took a while to gain friends because people
thought I was mean," he says. "I was kind of
a juvenile delinquent."

Shaquille (at lower right) hamming it up with some friends during his college days

He wasn't very devoted to his studies. "I used to be a class clown," he says. And, Shaquille felt bad about his size. He tried not to look so big. He hunched his shoulders. He didn't take much interest in sports. He wanted to dance on the television show "Fame" when he grew up. "My parents told me to be proud," he says. "But I wasn't. I wanted to be normal."

By the time he was 13, he was already 6 feet 8 inches tall. That made it pretty hard to look "normal." But Shaquille found that his size was good for basketball. And basketball helped him grow into his body.

Sergeant Harrison was stationed in Germany during that time. One day, basketball coach Dale Brown, from Louisiana State University, came to the base to hold a clinic.

**Shaquille hangs on to the rim after a slam dunk during a
college game.**

Shaquille went up to him. "I need a strength program, Coach Brown," he said. "I'm 6'8" and can't jump."

Coach Brown looked at Shaquille. "How long have you been in the army, soldier?"

"I'm not in the army," said Shaquille. "I'm only thirteen."

"Thirteen!" said Coach Brown. "Where's your dad?"

Coach Brown knew a prospect when he saw one. He became friends with the family. He gave Shaquille some tips. He decided to keep an eye on how Shaquille developed.

And Shaquille began to develop quickly. "In Germany, I used to get in trouble a lot," he says. "So instead of hanging out with all the rest of the guys, I said, 'Time for a change.' While they were hanging out, I used to go to the gym every day and play basketball with the GIs."

"I just wanted to play ball. My dad told me, 'See this ball. It could put food on your table and give you the finer things in life.' He was right. I just kept playing and I never gave up."

Shaquille began to apply himself at school. When the family moved back to the United States in 1987, Shaquille found he was becoming a leader.

"I started making my own decisions," says Shaquille. "I used to have friends who would drink and do drugs. But I wasn't going to do that. No matter what."

"I just didn't like it. If I don't like doing something, I won't do it. I don't care who's doing it. Most of the time people would talk about how it was cool to do stuff like that. If they thought I wasn't cool, fine. But I wasn't going to do drugs or drink."

Shaquille (center) was a star player at Cole High School in San Antonio, Texas.

★ ★ ★

In 1987, Sergeant Harrison was stationed at Fort Sam Houston in Texas. Shaquille enrolled at Cole High School in San Antonio. In his junior year, he led his team to a 32-1 record.

He was even better as a senior. He averaged 32 points, 22 rebounds, and 8 blocked shots a game. Cole went undefeated and won the state championship. Shaquille was named the most valuable player in two national all-star games. The scouts were impressed. Shaquille was the top high-school prospect in the nation. He graduated in 1989.

Coach Brown had kept tabs on Shaquille. He wanted him to come to Louisiana State University. Shaquille remembered Coach Brown and how friendly and helpful he had been. He agreed to attend LSU.

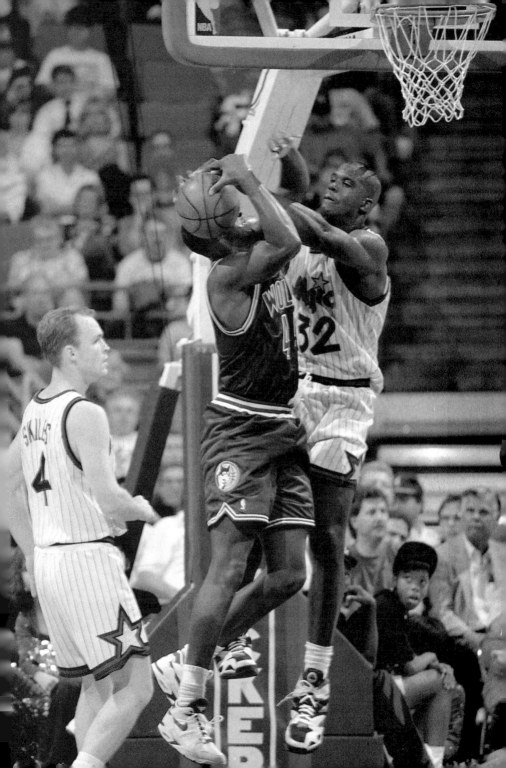

Shaquille worked hard at his classes and at adjusting to his new teammates. Because his family had moved so much, he had become an expert at making new friends. He adapted to the university and the town of Baton Rouge very quickly.

Shaquille averaged 13.9 points a game as a freshman. When he began his sophomore year, he felt settled and ready to show what he could really do. Early in the 1990-91 season, he scored 53 points in one game against Arkansas State. He averaged nearly 28 points a game for the year. He was named the best college player by *Sports Illustrated* magazine and the two major wire services, Associated Press and United Press International. People were now calling him just "Shaq." But a broken leg reminded him of how uncertain a career in sports could be.

The break wasn't bad—it was a stress fracture, and he was able to play on it until it healed—but it shook Shaquille up. The following year, opponents were doing almost anything to stop him. They knew that the only way to stop LSU was to stop Shaq. It wasn't any fun for Shaquille, and the thought of injury was in the back of his mind. Shaquille was a good student. He had nearly made the dean's list. His father had always wanted him to get a college degree. But Shaquille wondered whether a diploma was worth the risk. When LSU was eliminated from the annual college basketball tournament in the spring of 1992, Shaq decided to pass up his senior year and turn pro. His father supported his decision.

Shaquille dives hard for the ball during an LSU game.

The NBA allows all the teams that do not make the spring playoffs to have a shot at the top pick in the college draft. The Orlando Magic was the second-worst team in the league in 1991-92. They were an expansion team. The Magic had entered the NBA only two seasons before. The Magic won the lottery for the top pick.

Some people wondered whether Shaquille would want to play for an expansion team, especially one in Florida. It would be different than playing in New York or Chicago or Los Angeles, where Shaq would be sure to get a lot of attention.

Shaquille pointed out that Disney World was in Orlando. "I'm going to be chilling with Mickey," he said. He signed a contract worth $40 million and bought a house in the area. Sergeant Harrison planned to retire from the army and move the family to Orlando.

The attention would come to Shaquille.

Shaquille holds up his Orlando Magic jersey after being picked first in the 1992 NBA draft.

At the end of the 1992-93 season, Shaquille was named NBA Rookie of the Year.

Shaquille has already established himself in the NBA. In his first season, he made 56 percent of his shots and averaged 23.4 points, 13.9 rebounds, and 3.53 blocked shots a game. He was in the top 10 in the league in all of those categories. In fact, he was the only NBA player to place in the top 10 in any four statistical categories. Shaquille helped the Magic to have its best season so far. He earned a spot on the All-Star team as a rookie. Few people were surprised when, at the end of the season, Shaquille was named NBA Rookie of the Year.

Still, Shaquille is a humble player. After a game, he showers, then sits at his locker and answers the reporters' questions in his soft voice.

He surprises his teammates with how friendly and thoughtful he is. When Shaquille joined the team, Terry Catledge had Shaq's usual number, 33. Players often get attached to their numbers. But Shaq told his teammate to keep 33. He'd take number 32.

Shaquille knows that, no matter how good he is now, there's more work to be done. Says his coach, Matt Goukas, "People tend to forget how young he is because of how big he is. He's still learning the pro game. He doesn't really even know the language yet."

While growing up and in college, Shaq had always been the best player on his team. He had never been asked to set screens for his teammates, to allow them to get free for a shot. He had always been able to go to the hoop whenever he wanted. He needed to develop a jump shot and improve his free-throw shooting.

Readying for a free throw

"Shaquille is very graceful for his size," says Chamberlain. "I think this man is only going to get better and better, but he's going to have to be taught some inside skills. If he develops a little five-foot jumper, he's going to be tremendous."

"All he needs is that one shot, like Kareem had the sky hook," says Magic Johnson. "Then, look out."

Shaquille is just starting out and already he's being compared with the greatest centers in basketball history—Wilt Chamberlain and Abdul-Jabbar, with the great defensive player Bill Russell and the great all-around player Bill Walton. "I'm a fan," admits Shaquille. He enjoys talking with those Hall of Famers and hearing how they made themselves great.

"But I want to find out things for myself," says Shaquille. "Even though Bill Walton talks to me, they are his experiences, not mine. There was only one Bill Walton. Only one Russell. Only one Wilt. And there will be only one Shaq."

Chronology

1972 – Shaquille O'Neal is born in Newark, New Jersey.

1985 – At age 13, Shaquille meets Louisiana State University basketball coach Dale Brown during a basketball clinic at the army base in Germany where Shaquille's father is stationed.

1987 – Shaquille's father is transferred to Fort Sam Houston in Texas. Shaquille enrolls in Cole High School in San Antonio.

1989 – Cole goes undefeated and wins the state AAA championship. Shaquille averages 32 points, 22 rebounds and 8 blocked shots a game. He is named a Parade All-American and the most valuable player of the McDonald's All-Star Classic and the Dapper Dan Classic.
– Shaquille enrolls at LSU.

1990 – As a freshman, Shaquille averages 13.9 points a game and leads the Southeastern Conference in rebounds with an average of 12 per game.

1991 – Shaquille averages 27.6 points a game and is named
a first-team All-American. *Sports Illustrated*, the
Associated Press and United Press International name
him college player of the year. He is also honored as
SEC Athlete of the Year after becoming the first player
to lead the conference in scoring, rebounding, shooting
percentage, and blocked shots in the same season.

1992 – Shaquille averages over 24.1 points a game and
becomes the first player since Charles Barkley to lead
the SEC in rebounding three straight seasons. For his
career at LSU, he averages 21.6 points and 13.5
rebounds a game.
 – Shaquille turns pro and becomes the first player chosen
in the National Basketball Association draft. He is picked
by the Orlando Magic and signs a seven-year contract
worth an estimated $40 million.

1993 – Fans make Shaquille the first rookie since Michael Jordan
to be voted a starter in the All-Star Game. He finishes the
season with averages of 23.4 points, 13.9 rebounds, and
3.53 blocked shots per game, and is named the NBA's
Rookie of the Year.

★ ★ ★

About the Author

Ted Cox is a Chicago journalist who works at the *Daily Southtown*. He has covered sports for the Chicago *Reader* and *Chicago* magazine. He worked at United Press International and holds a B.S. in journalism from the University of Illinois at Urbana Champaign. He lives in Chicago with his wife, Catherine, and their daughter, Sadie.